When I Grow Up

Children's views of the adult world

compiled by

Claire Rayner

Virgin

Designed and produced by
Genesis Productions Limited
30 Great Portland Street, London W1N 5AD

First published in Great Britain 1986 by
Virgin Books
328 Kensal Road
London W10 5XJ

ISBN 0-86369-174-9

Designed by Jane Ewart
Research by Esther Jagger
Cover design by Christos Kondeatis

Printed and bound in Hong Kong by
Mandarin Offset Limited

WORK

FAMILY

DISCIPLINE

POLITICS

LOVES + HATES

LIFESTYLE

TV

OUR WORLD

HEAVEN

My small son, aged four, walked all round my extremely pregnant shape and asked, 'Is all of you my Mummy?' Startled, I assured him I was all of a piece – that I didn't come in slices – and he said appreciatively, 'Mm, what a lot of Mummy!'

I wish now, not for the first time, that I had a record other than my unreliable memory of all the other delightful things my children have said. I meant to write it down at the time, but you know how it is when you're a busy parent. There's so much to do, looking after children – and one day you wake up and discover someone has come along and stolen twenty years in the night and your 'little ones' are now grown-up ones. The dialogue changes and you've no record of the marvellously wise and funny and perceptive and sad and touching things they said to you while they did their growing.

That is the heart of this book – the things children say recorded now, while it's still new. There is so much that is precious in young minds, so much we ought to hear from them, for they have a view of the world which in its freshness and honesty can teach us a great deal. A child's view of government can be cruelly revealing and make us think again about what we want from those we elect to run our lives, and what we get. A child's comment on parenthood can be very beady-eyed and can make us think again about what sort of fist we're making of rearing the next generation to be the sort of adults we'd have liked to be ourselves. And a child's drawing of God can be rich with wisdom and make us think again about how little we actually think . . .

To get this book together, we needed the help of teachers – and we were given it in full measure and running over. All over the country busy schools were busier still as children wrote and drew items for inclusion in these pages. It would have been marvellous if we could have included all of them. There is so much that was sent to me that I simply couldn't use for lack of space and which I hated to leave out. For there was never lack of quality. So, to the teachers and to the children whose work they collected for me, my deepest thanks. They are the people who made this book, not me.

And it is important, of course, that the people who make a book should be rewarded in some way for doing so. And because it isn't practical to pay the children whose work is included in these pages, it is going to other children. Deprived ones, hungry ones, unhappy ones, and it is going to them via The Save the Children Fund.

I hope you enjoy this book. Actually, I don't see how you couldn't.

WORK

I want to be . . .

a policemen with a
hard truncheon

Jamie, 7

a private Investigator and solve
every bodys Problems like finding
murderers

David, 8

a police - lady
because I like
to catch the
naughty men

Deborah, 7

Girls shouldn't be police
officers because they
are unreliable.

Daniel, 8

Amanda, 8

this is me a policeman catching a burglars

Michael, 8

a farmer because of the smells and
I like the muk speader because I got
some in my face when i was small

Nathan, 8

I am going to
dig for
chemicles
on the
moon

Jonathan, 7

a secretary I would be smart
and I would get away
from my children
I would work
for the royal
family

Lisa, 10

a clown because then I will go in a circus and I'll Dress with a little hat with a flower and flopy feet.

Laura, 7

a parachatest

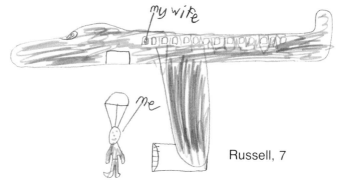

my wife

me

Russell, 7

I would like to go down the mining pit

Alicia, 11

I will never, ever become a miner. A job in Which people could be killed should be barred.

Andrew, 11

an aeroplane pilot Because I would like to give displays to lots of people.

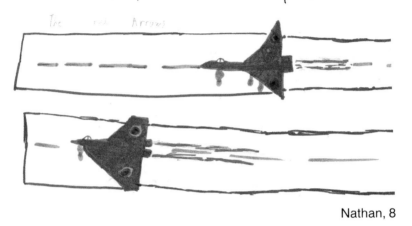

Nathan, 8

I will help people push there cars out of the mud.

Emma, 6

a waitress because I like to give dinners and drinks and puddings too

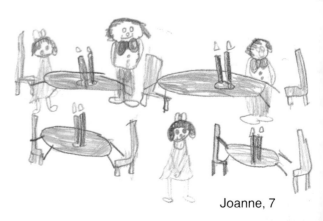

Joanne, 7

I am going to
be a pub lady
I am going to get
nice Jumpers

Charlotte, 6

Charmaine, 8

I would like to be an Astronomer when I grow up because I am keen on the subject and it is an excuse to stay up late at night, not to mention the use of all the infrared equipment and knowing more info than I do now.

Mark, 11

Michael, 8

a Vet because I love animals and the vet helps animals. Like if a cat had a disease he would give it Some pills

Victoria, 7

a Vet Because we've got a cat and a rabbit.

Jonathan, 7

woof

Timothy, 7

a Vet Shop

when I grow up I will Live on top of the vet place

Kirsty, 7

a fireman because
I like getting cats
that are on the roof
and put the fire out
and I would like
to go up the ladder

Lance, 7

firemen often see worse sights than a
patient in an operating theatre.

Andrew, 10

a fireman because
I always wanted to
hold a hose and put
the fire
down

Amar, 7

A Lollipop Lady

Faye, 4

a digger driver I would buy a digger and work for my self.

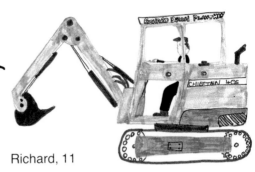

Richard, 11

Should men and women do the same work?
Yes, because . . .

its not farr if the boys have better fobs than the girls.

Charlie, 7

it would not befare to the girls but! when I played football against Manfield I was tackled by a girl and I thought I could go pass her.

Michael, 8

mummys might get fed up with cooking and daddys might get fed up with mending the car

Gemma, 8

women and men can do each others work if they try hard enough.

Jennifer, 9

No, because . . .

my dad makes my food go black.

Amy, 7

women don't like having muscles.

Iris, 8

boys and Girls should not do the same things because you are not alawd to copy people at school.

Katie, 8

boys and girls. should do different work.

Michelle, 7

Getting married means . . .

You have to hunt the streets for someone you fall in love with.

Emma, 6

having a hang-over the next morning.

Rundle, 10

doing washing up.

Victoria, 6

that you live with a lady.

Steven, 11

to move into a house and to have funiture and beds and Sofa and chairs.

Gemma, 7

Emma, 8

I think that man and women get together and be in piece.

Fiona, 10

a demanding husband and kids and a lot of work and nothing to show for it.

Maria, 11

you have to be ready to forgive.

Beth, 11

I want to get married because . . .

iF you have a BaBy and you are going to work the next Day, you have got a husbend to mind it.

Nicola, 10

so I could carry on the surname 'Young'.

Mark, 11

I like cooking and then I can have some children but if I didn't get Married I wouldn't have to buy So much food

Michael, 7

I don't want to get married because . . .

I do not like marrying and I have been thinking at home and I can't think of anybody to marry.

Andrew, 6

It makes me embarassed

Sean, 7

I would not leave my mum and Dad a lone

Noreen, 8

Cindy, 6

I don't know why but just the thought of it puts me off

Sarah, 11

I would like to marry . . .

someone who is strong so that she could push the car.

Matthew, 7

Erika because She is the same size

Paul, 6

an apserlotly dishy man

Nicola, 10

a modest, truthful man.

Clare, 11

I would go down on one knee and ask her to marry me and give her a rose.

Simon, 11

Daniel, 8

a nice women and I am going to buy a cat. I want a nice cat and I want her to be called Rose and she will have Rosee cheeks

Eric, 7

a woman with blond hair, blue eyes, no spots or Frekles, no guffy teeth, no gegs (glasses). No warts or corns, no verukas, no beard or maustache. No curly hair AND Sertanly not FAT.

Matthew, 11

a man who doesn't keep taking my money. I will let him do The washing up and cook me dinner

Angel, 6

Veronica, 7

George, 9

I think in marriage you
Shouldnt divorce my mummy
might divorce so daddy can
marry brenda Divorcing isn't
very nice for the children

Sarah, 6

Who will be the boss at home?

I think whoever puts the
most money towards the
house would be the boss.

Sharon, 11

My wife would be the
boss because if there is any
trouble she can sort it out.

Matthew, 10

No-one would be boss of the house
because we would run it like a
two person government.

Mark, 11

Where do babies come from?

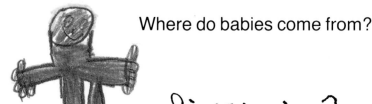

John, 7

firginia?

Claire, 10

from mummys tummys and when
I have a baby I hope it just
comes from my tummy not
some were else wandering around

Donna, 8

From girls and

god.

Glen, 7

Timothy, 7

you come from a sack full of water and first
you are a little seed and then you grow. as
you will see it is all verry complicated

Daniela, 7

DISCIPLINE

If my children always did as they were told . . .

I would think they were'nt normle

Joanne, 11

it would be impossieball

Elizabeth, 9

I would take them to disneyland but I would not do it everyday

Imogen, 8

FAIRGround

Emma, 7

If my children were rude or naughty . . .

They would have to do the washing up and police thier shoas

Angus, 9

I would punish them, they can get into big trouble like is you insult a police man you could get put in prison

Lee, 11

I would smack my little girl and send her to bed But I would give her some breakfast and some dinner and some supper

Stacey Anne, 8

What are policemen for?

to catch Stranger's

Mushir, 8

to Stop fights vadilisam and roits

Michelle, 10

They help children if they are lost and they look for accidends

Zahid, 9

Christopher, 8

to keep us safe from Nutters

Duncan, 11

for stopping killing and drugs and for looking smart in their uniforms

Lavinia, 9

Matthew, 10

What are teachers for?

so they can learn us work

Jamie, 11

If we were taught by our mums and dads one part of the population might be using millimetres, another inches and the other centimetres so we would not fully understand each other

Mark, 11

The Winner is the pe with H most pon

$2 \times 12 =$
$12 \times 2 =$
$100 + 10 =$
$6 \times 6 =$

six of cut out so 90 off now page away

Emma, 6

to make sure everyone can read and write

Kirsteen, 11

I would get enjoyment teaching younger children And see their character develop as they begin to learn

Joanne, 10

POLITICS

What does the government do?

closes and opens and closes places

Paul, 9

fight over who is going to be Prime Minister next

Michelle, 10

If there wasn't a government we would all be higgly pigly

Juliana, 9

sit on ther backsides and smoke cigars

Daniel, 8

pay the uninploed

Kirsteen, 11

I don't think they do much to help anybody except themselves

Xavier, 11

If I ran the government . . .

I would make the oil, paraffin, petrol and other fuels so that only the rich could afford them so that They wont run out so fast and the poor people could have log fires fitted in every room cheaply and more people could have Jobs as lumber Jack's

Paul, 8

I would grow lots of flowers

Anthony, 6

Lucy, 7

I would ban drug's cigarettes glue sniffing cruelty to animals and to stop people killing foxe's

Suzanne, 8

I would lower the price of holidays because they are lovely

Lavinia, 9

I would change alot of thing Like starting wars

Daniel, 10

Why do wars happen?

because one Country Sees one Side of the argument and another Country Sees the other Side So they fight

Lynn, 10

There is no real reason for the wars to happen

Xavier, 11

war would mean that I had to try and kill somebody and if I did it would hang round me like a ghost

Heather, 11

the best thing that could happen to me is to win a war

Andrew, 11

Richard, 11

I wouldn't like to fight in a war but I would tend to the wounded

Christine, 10

Jennifer, 8

People dont think about the fact that we children have to live through the situations they make

Andrew, 11

LOVES + HATES

I would like to . . .

do the gardening because I like to find worms and scare people

Andrew, 6

do the washing because I get my fingers wrinkly

Sarah, 7

iron because I cuddle the warm clothes

Gemma, 7

I wouldn't like to . . .

grow up like my sister's, they smoke and hang around late at night

Lorna, 10

kiss because I don't like it

Craig, 7

I will never . . .

kill my children or any other people because I was a brownie

Melissa, 7

marry a girl from our school

Richard, 10

go about glue-sniffing because you can go crazy and kill some-body or you can kill your self

Paul, 11

NEVER TAKE Drugs

Don't Smoke

Paul, 10

build a house No No No No I will not build a house because it is dangerous and I can drop the brick on my foot and I will scream

Rebecca, 7

The best thing that could happen to me . . .

win The bingo

Tracy, 11

whould be one of my books becoming a best seller Then I could buy a old castel

Nicholas, 11

Susan, 7

that I might get a Job very Quickly

Parminder, 10

The worst thing that could happen to me . . .

I might lose my teddy

Lavinia, 9

would be to get a disease like cancer

Beth, 11

if my wife left and it Snowed all year

Matthew, 10

if my dad and mum died and I had to go into a home

Denise, 11

The clothes I should like to wear . . .

snooKer clothes a wast-coat blacK trousers a White shirt and a bow tie and blacK shoes

Jamie, 7

Amy, 7

the kind of clothes David Bowie likes to wear

Roland, 10

I couldnt care less what I Wear. This does not mean I Would dress up like a flower to go to Work is I get a job

Andrew, 11

This is me I am a Punk I think I would like to grow up like this. But My mum would shot at me Porbably

Elizabeth, 9

I'm going to be a punk rocker

Lance, 7

Jason, 8

I like
laced
clothes

Victoria, 6

I will like to keep up with the fashon when I'm older. But I don't know if the clothes I've drawn will be the fashon when I'm grown up

Nicola, 11

in the most modern house there is with green roses. In the kitchen there would be a microwave and the food would be 21st century mush, there will be liquidised gunge in all different colours. There will be no electricity because there's going to be solar panels on the roof

Roland, 10

I want a neit and tidy house I want red curtains a cat and Pink shoes

Susan, 6

Where I will live

Iain, 9

I will live in
a hotel with ten
thousand Rooms and
an atic with a
cafe and a puB

Matthew, 7

I am going to live in a light house
by the side of the red sea

Daniel, 7

the best thing that could happen
to me is to be a millionaire
and live in a mansion and I
would pay the council to put
a swimming pool in the
back yard

Tony, 11

In the kitchin I want ten
mickrawave ovens six
frezzers and seven table's
and glowing lights

Suzanne, 8

I want a big
grenaderer and
a big expensive
house

Thomas, 7

Alex, 7

Television is . . . .

for children who can't read the News parper

Julia, 7

for Waching your very very very Best childrens Programmes because in the BOOKs The pictures dont move

Emma, 8

Some one giving the Sports news

Thomas, 5

to watch and keep you happy and sad

Tanya, 10

Apostolos, 5

for when you are bored
It puts Some Action in your life Richard, 10

to give you
information
and Sometimes
it can
branewash
you

Dimple, 8

Louise, 8

If I were on television . . .

I would be a guest on breakfast
television and be cool and wear a
giant white glimmering grin

Roland, 10

I d tell about polution
and dumping in woods

Scott, 9

Kirsty, 7

I would act
if I was a
actress and
I would not
stand there

Dimple, 8

I would Make a stunt
Movie because I like
stunts. Me and Oliver
do stunts on his
bed and they are
brilliant stunts

Nathan, 8

Mark, 11

I would make flims about love
and murder and it would
have three parts

Deirdre, 11

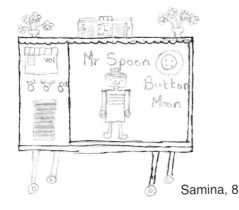

Samina, 8

I whud be
skered and
run out

Kevin, 8

OUR WORLD

If people can't find work . . .

there brain goes rustey

Timothy, 7

they go roaming the steets and
when they have had enough of
that they go and watch
television and when they have had
enough of that they go and look
in the larder and there is
nothing there and they die

Amy, 7

Michelle, 7

I think that everyone should have a job and the gouverment should do some thinking about it

Mushir, 10

Cindy, 6

they become gipsies and they travel around the world

Jamie, 7

If you do not find any work then you could help peope do things like the old and the disabled

Kate, 10

It's not fair . . .

that people should have no homes

Christine, 10

to eat cattle and lambs

Suzanne, 8

we have lovely food and
some ^where^ about the other
side of the world people
are starving to death

Sarah, 7

that people are put in prison
for some thing they Havent done

Roger, 9

When the teachers get treated badly

Christine, 11

They kill elephants just
for their tusks

Sarah, 9

I don't think the apartheid is fair

Beth, 11

It is not fair on blind def and disabled

Paul, 11

The government spends tons of money on an underground tunnel to france, but people in Ethiopia die

Andrew, 11

What I would do about famines . . .

I would make underwater towns and cities. Under water there are loads of fish

Richard, 10

Jane, 6

I would raise money to buy food
by selling my paintings

Rachael, 11

Some people would buy a
mansion with 1,000,000 rooms
and not spare a thought for
people in Africa

Andrew, 11

I would give them money
oh I forgot they have
no shops I would send
bread and eggs

Kevin, 7

I will give them
blankets and a sleeping bags
and I will give them
clothes and shose
and socses

Rickey, 8

Growing old . . .

Old people look like this : totally white hair, wrinkles galore, veins showing up like cats eyes on a dark night on their wrists, No make up, gnarled fingers, old fashioned clothes (about the seventies sort), and sometimes deaf but nearly always got false choppers.

Mark, 11

I will enjoy being old because people help you alot and they care for you by giving you big easter eggs

Jennifer, 9

I would not like to get old because then you're afraid of dying

Rachael, 11

Roland, 10

What happens when people die?

you are put in a coffin with a pillow of sawdust and have a long sleep

Lavinia, 9

After youre gone through the gates of Heaven everything is like Paradise (well it is really) there are televisions and videos everywhere and everything is FREE! If you get bored of watching T.V. you can go and visit God and he'll reincarnate you as whatever you want

Roland, 10

Sometimes we think God is unkind if someone dies but we have to make room for other people

Beth, 11

Thoughts on God . . .

I think god has a beard that stretches round the universe

Richard, 10

god is not a person or a thing He just has two eyes in a calender

Shahbaz, 6

God is very old I think he wears a white headband with a Checked jacket

Matthew, 10

God is owner of the World

Clive, 9

In heaven theres cats everywhere and Henry is sitting on a throne made of gold. People fuss cats in Heaven and live second lives

Rachael, 11

God is Talking to Jesus

Paul, 8

God invents all our friends and adults

Emma, 8

God is mixed—
a man and a woman

Lateef, 7

Michael, 8

If God sees someone being bad to people he makes the thunder come

Anthony, 6

Allah helps you to be nice

Samar, 7

He does make it rain and make the wind and a lot of other bits of weather

Leesa, 10

He is supposed to be the Earths creator. He is supposed to control life on Earth But I'm not really sure

Peter, 10

God

God plays center forward FoR EverTon

Darren, 11

David, 8

Save the Children

Save the Children fights hard and constantly on behalf of children who start life with the odds very unfairly stacked against them. The Fund was set up some seventy years ago to help Austrian victims of the First World War, and now its activities range worldwide.

Every day 40,000 children die from disease and malnutrition. Few of those who survive will receive proper food, health care or education. Even in Britain poverty, unemployment and poor housing place great stress on many families.

With the help of people like you, the readers of this book, and of the children who made it all possible, Save the Children can help less privileged children lead the kind of lives they deserve. But it all needs money – lots of money, all the time.

£1 buys enough polio vaccine to protect ten children from this crippling disease; £5 provides a nourishing meal for twenty hungry children in India. You have already helped by buying this book. If you would like to give more, please send your donation to:

Save the Children
17 Grove Lane
London SE5 8RD
(Telephone 01-703 5400)

(Photo: Penny Tweedie/Save the Children)

Education for children in a Bangladeshi village.

Immunization in Uganda.

(Photo: Chris Steele-Perkins/Save the Children)